The Squirrel Who Ate All The Nuts

By Lisa Dunbar

The Belcher's Press

Lindside, W

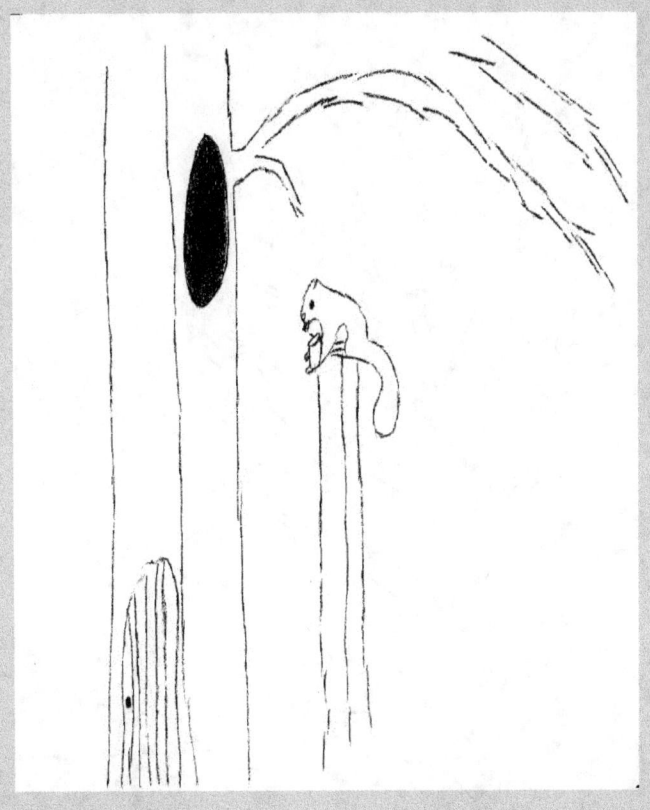

There once was a squirrel named
Simi who liked to eat all the
nuts.

Simi would hide here nor
there. Behind trees nor bushes.

When Simi found a tree
that had some nuts no matter
what kind they were.

He would stuff all the nuts
in his mouth and would gobble
them all down.

The squirrels in the forest couldn't help but wonder what happened to all the nuts in the forest. None could come up with an answer

One squirrel shouted
"Simi's been eaten all the nuts."
"What are we going to do?"
another squirrel shouted.

Simi heard all the talking
and worry from the other
squirrels.

That made Simi feel bad.

So Simi went to where he
hid the giant stash of nuts.

And so Simi shared the
nuts that he had taken from
every tree in the froest with all of
the other squirrels.

From there on Simi and all the other squirrels shared their nuts and gathered them up for the winter.

Not only would they share there nuts among one another. But they would also help each other build their homes.

Then when the harsh winters came they had enough food put pack so none of them would go hungry.

Then they decided to lay
back in the winter and they had
plenty of food to eat. Along with
a place to stay. They watched

the snow and hoped for spring to
come.

≈Notes≈